# The Solitude Code

## Cracking the Secrets of Personal Power

Dilasha Adhikari

Healing is not about You Forgetting your Past.

Healing is you still remembering everything and not getting triggered by your Past.

Dilasha Adhikari

In our minds' sky, the fear of being alone looms large like a storm cloud. It is normal to experience it and to harbour these qualms and concerns. Pay close attention, though, because I want to show you how to use that fear to your advantage.

Imagine a vast, peaceful forest. You are at the edge, watching the sunbeams play hide-and-seek through the leaves. Being alone may resemble entering that wilderness in that it is uncharted and possibly intimidating. But keep in mind that every forest has its own form of magic.

Dilasha Adhikari

But what if I get lost in there? you may be asking. What if I am unable to escape? These ideas act as the underbrush that seeks to obstruct your way. But I can assure you that you will discover paths in that solitary woodland that you were unaware even existed.

It's like holding a mirror to your heart when you're by yourself. Without any covers or pretences, you can see who you really are. And guess what? You are wonderful in every way. Finding a treasure of self-love and self-acceptance within oneself is like finding it when you appreciate your own company.

*Dilasha Adhikari*

Undoubtedly, there may be times when your fear grabs you a little more tightly. Like a breeze, it rustles the forest's leaves. Remember, though, that you're not the only one who experiences that fear.

It accompanies being human. The trick is to use it as fuel to spark your inner strength rather than letting it paralyze you.

*Dilasha Adhikari*

Imagine a bird perched high on a branch. Before anything can soar, it must first make a leap.
In a similar vein, making the decision to overcome your fear of being by yourself is that leap for you. It is about having the courage to move on in spite of your fear, not about getting rid of it. You'll discover that you can fly higher than you ever imagined as you do this.

Don't close the door on your fear when it comes knocking at your heart's door. Invite it inside and engage in dialogue with it. Tell it that even if it's a part of you, it doesn't have any power over you. You are the navigator of your own vessel and the discoverer of your own forest.

*Dilasha Adhikari*

And as you enter that lonely wilderness and face your anxiety there, you'll come out the other side stronger, wiser, and more attuned to your own needs than you could have ever thought. You'll come to understand that being alone isn't anything to fear; rather, it's a voyage of self-discovery that brings you to the lovely realization that you are sufficient in your own uniqueness.

*Dibasha Adhikari*

# About Author

Dilasha Adhikari is a woman who persevered through hardship and trauma. She experienced moments of seclusion and loneliness as a result of the hardships she faced in life. She discovered the deepest truths about herself, though, in these seemingly lonely places.

Through reflection, self-awareness, and the calm reflection that solitude allowed, Dilasha Adhikari rose from the depths of her own troubles as a transformed person. Her experience came to serve as a symbol of the value of valuing personal time alone for growth, learning, and healing.

Dilasha Adhikari is committed to reaching out to others and providing them with the support and inspiration they need with an unyielding commitment.

*Dilasha Adhikari*

Her life experiences have inspired her desire to motivate and uplift others by showing them how to overcome obstacles, realize their full potential, and embrace the light that resides inside.

She invites readers to travel with her through her words on a journey of empowerment, healing, and self-discovery. Her experience serves as a powerful reminder that each person has the ability to overcome obstacles no matter how difficult the circumstances may seem. Be prepared to be inspired, lifted up, and urged to believe in your own potential despite life's difficulties and embrace solitude as you read through the pages of her book.

*Dilasha Adhikari*

# Content:

1. Overview
2. Introduction
3. Mind Body and Heart
4. Definition of Solitude
5. Importance of Being Alone
6. The Benefits of Being Alone
7. Overcoming the Fear of Being Alone
8. Finding Comfort In Solitude
9. Self-Reflection and Personal Development
10. Building Meaningful Relationship
11. How to be Mindful When You Are Alone
12. Conquering Your Inner Demons
13. Embracing Creativity and Imagination: The Pathway to Self-Expression
14. How to encourage Creativity and Imagination
15. Lessons For Life From Using Imagination and Creativity
16. Cultivating Gratitude and Appreciation
17. How to develop gratitude and appreciation
18. Lessons For Life From Developing Gratitude and Appreciation

*Dilasha Adhikari*

19. Lessons for Life Including Alone Time

20. Understanding Yourself

21. Discover Your Passion

22. Setting Goals and Taking Actions

23. Understanding the Value of Personal Space

    In a Relationship (Finding Room to Breathe)

24. Solitude- A Sanctuary For Healing and Self Care

25. Overcoming Trauma and Finding Solace in Solitary Moments

26. Seeking Solitude In the Digital World

27. Exploring the connection between Solitude and spirituality

28. Tips For Incorporating Solitude into Daily Life

29. The Profound Impact of Solitude and its lasting benefits

30. Spirituality and Solitude: Deepening Your Connection

    with the Universe

31. Overcoming Social Pressure: Embracing Your Authentic Self

32. The Power Of Silence

33. Creating a Balanced Life:

    Integrating Solitude with Social Engagement

34. Encouragement and Guidance to embark on Your Own

    Solitary Journey

*Dilasha Adhikari*

# Overview

The book "The Solitude Code" explores how solitude has the power to transform. We frequently have the feeling of being constantly surrounded by people and inundated with noise and distractions in today's fast-paced and highly connected society. What if, however, we made the effort to tune out of the outside world and commune with our inner selves? What if we accepted solitude as a chance for development and self-discovery?

*Dilasha Adhikari*

This book serves as a manual for discovering the strength of solitude. It examines the advantages of solitude and offers helpful advice on how to make the most of your alone time. It explores the psychological and emotional effects of being alone, addressing common anxieties and uncertainties and offering solutions. This book is for you whether you are an extrovert or an introvert, whether you are on your healing journey or enjoy being alone or find it intimidating. Giving you the skills and direction you need to connect with your inner self, get rid of limiting ideas, and lead a more fulfilled life, it will assist you in realizing your full potential. Therefore, this book is your guide if you're ready to appreciate the power of solitude.

*Dilasha Adhikari*

# Introduction

Have you experienced feeling disoriented and unsure about your identity or your goals in life? Have you ever discovered that you put other people's pleasure and well-being ahead of your own by continually seeking their affirmation and approval? If so, you're not the only one.

It's simple to get distracted by the noise and diversions of daily living in today's fast-paced and connected world. We are continuously subjected to messages about what we ought to believe, do, and live our lives. We frequently gauge our sense of worth by looking outside of ourselves at things like our jobs, our relationships, and our assets.

*Dilasha Adhikari*

But would you believe I told you that there is a method to overcome these restrictive thoughts and get in touch with your own self? What if I told you that you possess the ability to change your life and that all it takes to do so is to spend some time by yourself?

Many of us find the idea of being alone to be frightening. We have been socialized to think that in order to be content and happy, we need other people. But what if we saw solitude as a chance for personal development? What if we made the most of our alone time by getting in touch with our thoughts, feelings, and intuition in order to identify our genuine interests and purposes in life?

*Dilasha Adhikari*

We shall examine the value of solitude and how it might improve your life in this book. We'll go deeper into the process of self-discovery and investigate the advantages of solitude, including improved self-awareness, a clearer sense of purpose, and a closer bond with our inner selves. We'll also talk about the difficulties of living alone, like loneliness and isolation, and offer solutions for overcoming these difficulties.

*Dilasha Adhikari*

So join me as we explore the power of being alone if you're prepared to set out on a voyage of self-discovery and establish a connection with your actual self.

Alongside, we will discover how to cherish solitude, take time to think back on the past, pinpoint our basic beliefs, connect with our passions, and ultimately live a more honest and fulfilled life.

For many of us, being alone can be frightening and terrifying. Our culture promotes social interaction, and the thought of being alone is frequently associated with negativity. However, spending time alone may be a transforming experience that helps us get to know ourselves better and uncover our true selves. In this book, we'll examine the value of solitude and how it can support our quest for self-awareness and personal development.

*Dilasha Adhikari*

I want to Pretend
I live in Invisible
World.
Let Them see me
But I won't.
I will guard my
Heart and Mind
Until the day
everything is Fine

*Dilasha Adhikari*

# Mind, Body and Heart

Before discussing solitude and its potential benefits, we must first improve our understanding of how our body, mind and heart work.

Spending time alone is like rest for our hearts and minds, just as we need sleep to rest our bodies. We can actually hear what is happening inside when we take a break from the chaos outside. It gives us a chance to revitalize and feel closer to ourselves.

*Dilasha Adhikari*

Let's picture your life as a mesmerizing dance that requires all of your mental, physical, and emotional resources. These parts work together to generate a fascinating choreography; each executes its own special moves while also depending on the other parts. Your mind is the planner and thinker. It analyzes data, works out issues, and directs your course of action. It manages every move in this complex dance as the conductor.

Your body is the vehicle through which your ideas and emotions are physically expressed. You move forward in the world, absorbing its textures and facing its difficulties.

*Dilasha Adhikari*

The dancer is what makes the choreography come to life, and that dancer is you.

You have the power to change the choreography. All it takes is one moment to realize.

The emotional core of your body is the heart. It's where your emotions live, where passions erupt, and where relationships are built. The dance is fueled by music, which gives it life and dimension.

*Dilasha Adhikari*

The intellect, body, and heart are linked throughout life. They are interdependent, influencing and reacting to each other's every move. Imagine a dance in which the heart adds joy and the body carries out the plan to leap. This dance isn't always precisely synced, which is the twist. The expectations, demands, and chaos of daily life might disrupt the rhythm.

That's where solitude enters the stage. The dance's stop, or intermission, is solitude. It's a location where the body, mind, and heart may come together, reset, and reconnect. You offer them an opportunity to communicate, comprehend one another's movements, and rediscover their rhythm in the middle of seclusion.

*Dilasha Adhikari*

When you are alone, you can clear your mind of clutter, relax your body, and hear your heart's whispers. There is a pause in the dance, like a calm clearing, where the dancers can coordinate their moves.

Instead of implying isolation, solitude invites self-discovery. It holds the key to solving the riddles that frequently get buried behind the din of modern life. You discover insights that direct your steps on the dance floor of life when you give your mind, body, and heart the chance to synchronize.

*Dilasha Adhikari*

So accept isolation as an essential partner in this dance of existence. Make it the place where your body, mind, and heart may interact, align, and dance in harmony. You'll discover the solutions you're looking for, the clarity you long for, and the rhythm that transforms the performance of your life into a work of incredible beauty in this dance.

*Dilasha Adhikari*

# Definition of Solitude

It's simple to conjure up feelings of isolation, loneliness, and even terror when we think of being alone. We have been socialized to think that being alone is undesirable and should be avoided at all costs. But what if we took a different perspective on solitude?

What if we viewed it as a chance for personal development and growth? What if we saw isolation as a means of achieving genuine inner fulfilment?

*Dilasha Adhikari*

So here is my version that defines being alone/in solitude,

Being alone is spending time alone, apart from other people. It might have been an accident or a conscious decision. It's possible to be alone in many different ways, such as on a solitary mountain trek, on a calm evening spent reading a book, or just by yourself in solitude thinking. But in any case, spending time with yourself offers a chance to get to know oneself better.

*Dilasha Adhikari*

Finding the time and space to think, rest, and connect with your inner self are the fundamental goals of being by yourself. It's about turning inward to examine your own ideas, feelings, and desires while taking a vacation from the noise and distractions of the outside world. Finding your own voice and paying attention to your intuition is key. We can explore a vast array of possibilities when we learn to love being by ourselves. We give ourselves the time and space to consider our prior encounters, define our key principles, and go further into our hobbies and passions. When we are continuously surrounded by others, it is impossible for us to connect with our inner selves. Being alone enables us to become more self-aware, to become more clear about our objectives and aims, and to eventually live a more genuine and satisfying life.

*Dilasha Adhikari*

However, living alone isn't always simple. To face our inner demons, worries, and insecurities in the open might be frightening. Sitting with our own thoughts and feelings, particularly those that are unpleasant or challenging to process, can be uncomfortable. Additionally, it might be difficult to maintain the discipline and drive necessary to make the most of our alone time.

Being alone is a decision in the end. Disconnecting from the outside noise and reestablishing contact with oneself are choices. Prioritizing our personal growth and well-being is a decision, even if it requires venturing outside of our comfort zones. To embrace the power of solitude and find our genuine selves requires a choice. So, the next time you find yourself by yourself, seize the chance. Who knows what you could learn about yourself along the way?

*Dilasha Adhikari*

# Importance of Being Alone

Ever felt alienated from yourself or lost? Do you feel like you're just going through the motions of life with no real direction or purpose? If so, perhaps it's time to enjoy yourself alone.

Being alone is not always easy. It occasionally can be frightening, uncomfortable, and even painful. We can, however, fully connect with ourselves and reclaim our sense of purpose during those solitary moments.

*Dilasha Adhikari*

It's challenging to hear our inner voice when we're surrounded by noise and distractions all the time. We lose focus on what is truly essential to us when we become enmeshed in other people's ideas and expectations.

But when we are alone, we can shut out the cacophony and re-establish contact with our authentic selves. We can think about the past, present, and future during those reflective times. We may delve into our deepest motivations and discover what makes us truly happy. We can access our creativity by paying attention to our intuition. Even better, we can simply remain with our feelings and thoughts, letting ourselves experience whatever arises without restriction or outside distraction.

*Dilasha Adhikari*

However, the benefits of solitude go beyond personal growth. Self-care is also a key component. We can become spent and fatigued when we're surrounded by others all the time. We may recharge our batteries and return to the world feeling renewed and energized by setting aside time for solitude.

We can face our anxieties and insecurities when we are alone, which is maybe the most essential benefit. Our inner demons come out to play during those times of seclusion.

*Dilasha Adhikari*

Moreover, by taking them head-on, we can triumph over them and develop into better, more self-assured versions of ourselves.

So, whether you're feeling disoriented, cut off, or simply exhausted, don't be scared to appreciate being by yourself. Although it's not always simple, it's worthwhile. You'll emerge from it with a fresh sense of direction and a stronger sense of self.

*Dilasha Adhikari*

They say Healing is a
Journey,
But they don't say Healing
is a Pain.
Healing is a Surrender,
Healing is a Game.
It takes time to numb that
Pain
And You can not take the
Shortest Lane

*Dilasha Adhikari*

# The Benefits Of Being Alone

Even while the idea of being alone can be frightening for some, it's crucial to realize that there are numerous advantages to spending time by yourself. In this chapter, we'll examine some of the major benefits of solitude, such as the chance to reflect on our feelings and thoughts free from interruptions, the chance to develop self-awareness and self-discovery, and the capacity to refuel and concentrate on personal development.

*Dilasha Adhikari*

## 1) Self Reflection:

It might be challenging to tune into our own thoughts and feelings when we are continuously surrounded by noise and distractions. However, having some alone time allows us to reflect on our inner selves without being interrupted by anything outside of ourselves. We might reflect on our past experiences and how they have shaped us, our current situation and how we feel about it, as well as our aspirations and objectives for the future. In order to make better decisions that are consistent with our values and objectives, reflection enables us to get clarity on what we genuinely need and desire in life.

*Dilasha Adhikari*

Do you ever feel like you have so much going on in your life—school, work, friends, and so forth—that you hardly have time to consider what's going on inside your own head? So, this is where self-reflection is useful. It's similar to pausing the video and checking in with yourself. Just how do I feel? What's my destination?

Imagine it as a mental health examination. Self-reflection is similar to visiting the doctor to ensure that your body is in good shape; it's like examining your thoughts and feelings. It's a chance to organize all the ideas and emotions that might be jumbled up inside.

*Dilasha Adhikari*

In Solitude, you can do a lot of things by yourself. You may sit and let your thoughts wander or you could read a book, listen to music, take a walk, etc. It's similar to granting yourself permission to operate on your own and it's possible that you'll come up with some intriguing ideas or thoughts during these times. It's like your brain has the opportunity to get some exercise and explore.

Self-reflection acts as your ally in healing. It's that specific period of time you set aside to sit down and talk to yourself. I think you should consider it an assessment of your emotional wounds. You pause and softly inquire, "How am I feeling? What's the matter? How can I make myself feel better?

Dilasha Adhikari

## 2) Self-awareness:

We have the chance to develop self-awareness while we are alone ourselves. Without any outside influences, we can genuinely tune into our own thoughts, feelings, and behaviours while we're alone ourselves. This self-awareness enables us to recognize areas in our life where we might need to make adjustments or improvements as well as to better understand ourselves and our own needs. By developing self-awareness, we can live more deliberately and make decisions that are consistent with our goals and ideals.

Being self-aware is similar to peering inside your own mind and emotions with a flashlight. Realizing the reasons behind your feelings and how you respond to certain situations takes time.

*Dilasha Adhikari*

Think of it as closely examining the mechanisms that drive you.

Self-awareness serves as your compass while you're recovering. Asking "Why am I feeling this pain?" in an honest manner is important. What makes me depressed or miserable?

Consider self-awareness as removing the onion's layers one layer at a time. In an effort to understand your sentiments more deeply, you delve deeper into your thoughts and feelings. You might discover certain habits you've formed to deal with pain or protect yourself. You may decide whether or not these habits are still beneficial to you by becoming aware of them.

*Dilasha Adhikari*

You might identify repeated patterns in your thoughts and actions while you spend time alone. You might find that you're frequently too harsh on yourself or that you tend to mistrust yourself more than you should. These insights are like finding lost treasure. Once you're aware of them, you may focus on changing your perspective and being kinder to yourself.

Spend some time becoming aware of yourself and learning about your emotions and responses. Find comfort in solitude and give yourself room to develop and change. The more you understand your inner workings, the more empowered you are to recover and grow stronger. Keep in mind that healing takes time.

*Dilasha Adhikari*

## 3) Self-discovery:

Being by oneself gives us the chance to become more self-aware and to learn new things about ourselves. Without any external demands or expectations, we are free to pursue our interests and passions when we are by ourselves. We can explore new interests, test out various pastimes, and discover what genuinely makes us happy and fulfilled. We can have more meaningful and fulfilling lives by learning more about ourselves.

Self-discovery is similar to going on an internal treasure hunt. It involves searching deeply inside your mind and emotions for the unique qualities that make you who you are. Consider it as re-learning who you are in a more profound and meaningful way.

*Dilasha Adhikari*

Self-discovery serves as your compass while you're recuperating. It involves looking into your feelings, dreams, and scars. Imagine shedding light on the recesses of your spirit that you may not have recently explored. What truly makes me happy, you may be asking yourself? What do I find most compelling? What phobias do I have?

Imagine releasing the weight of an old garment by peeled-away layers of outdated assumptions and ideals. Finding new aspects of oneself is what self-discovery is all about. It's about better comprehending prior wounds in order to heal them. Maybe you'll find behaviours that stemmed from suffering, or you'll recognize that some of your anxieties weren't as significant as you thought. Perhaps you can recall instances in which you showed courage or moments in which you shocked yourself with your fortitude.

*Dilasha Adhikari*

You can revisit these memories and experience the feelings that go along with them in solitude. It's similar to allowing your heart to breathe.

You might identify patterns in your feelings and responses as you spend time alone. You can find that you've been clinging to ideas that are no longer helpful to you. These awakenings are like completing the puzzle of who you are by finding the missing pieces. When you are aware of these components, you can work on rearranging them to develop a more attractive and genuine version of yourself.

Find comfort in solitude and give yourself time to feel and recover. Remember that healing is not only about correcting what is wrong.

It's also about uncovering the power, resiliency, and beauty that has always been inside of you.

*Dilasha Adhikari*

### 4) Improving oneself:

The ability to concentrate on personal growth and development is another benefit of being alone. It's easy to lose focus on our own needs and priorities when we're continuously surrounded by other people. However, spending time and space by ourselves allows us to concentrate on our own needs and personal development. In order to reach our goals, we can set objectives, make strategies on how to get there and focus on picking up new abilities or routines. We can improve ourselves and lead more happy lives by putting a strong emphasis on personal development.

Therefore, self-improvement is equivalent to providing yourself the opportunity to update, just like you would with a computer or phone. Making minor adjustments to your thoughts, behaviour, and lifestyle will help you become even better. Consider it as a wonderful portrait of your future self.

*Dilasha Adhikari*

You might begin to notice some habits that are limiting you while you're alone, such as being lethargic or doubting your abilities. It's similar to discovering rocks in your route that you can kick out of the way. Once you're aware of what's getting in your way, you may start making changes to your bad habits. Cleaning your ideas and deeds is similar to cleaning your room.

So, consider spending time alone if you're trying to improve yourself. Planning your personal development there is similar to having your own thought space. Spend some time alone thinking about what you've done and making new ambitions. Just keep in mind that isolation is the calm place where you can arrange the pieces of your puzzle of self-improvement.

*Dilasha Adhikari*

In conclusion, being alone has numerous advantages for us, such as the chance to cultivate self-awareness and self-discovery, the chance to reflect on our thoughts and feelings free from outside interruptions, and the capacity to refuel and concentrate on our own progress. We can strengthen our relationship with ourselves and build a more meaningful and purposeful life by learning to enjoy being by ourselves.

*Dilasha Adhikari*

# Overcoming The Fear Of Being Alone

The struggle to overcome loneliness anxiety is real. Addressing our deepest fears and insecurities demands courage, vulnerability, and a desire to do so. Being alone with our thoughts and feelings may be intimidating, difficult, and downright frightening for many of us. We can be afraid of what we might learn about ourselves or fear that we won't be able to endure the solitude's accompanying calm and stillness.

But it's crucial to keep in mind that fear is a normal reaction to the unknown. Our body uses it as a defence against perceived danger. The things we are most afraid of, however, are frequently not at all hazardous. In fact, they might be the same elements that enable our transformation, learning, and growth.

*Dilasha Adhikari*

Using mindfulness techniques is one of the best strategies to get over the anxiety of being by yourself. The practice of mindfulness involves being in the present without bias or attachment. When we engage in mindfulness practices, we develop the ability to observe our thoughts and feelings without getting sucked into them. This has the potential to be immensely liberating because it enables us to step back from our worries and view them for what they truly are.

Reframing our negative beliefs is a further method for conquering the anxiety of being alone. We might decide to regard solitude as a chance for development and self-discovery rather than as a cause of fear and anxiety. We might remind ourselves that being alone oneself gives us the time to consider our lives, develop objectives, and make significant changes.

*Dilasha Adhikari*

Reframing unfavourable thoughts is another method. When we think negatively about being alone, such as "I'm so lonely" or "No one wants to be around me," we can confront and reframe those views. We can tell ourselves things like, "I may be alone, but that doesn't make me worthless or undeserving of a relationship." We may shift the way we view things and lessen our dread of feeling alone by rephrasing negative thoughts.

Bear in awareness that combating the fear of being alone is an endeavour that calls for time and patience. As you embark on your path, be empathetic and sensitive to yourself. You can learn how to appreciate the endurance of solitary and arrive at peace with your own unique beauty with patience and diligence.

*Dilasha Adhikari*

# Finding Comfort In Solitude

We will all have times of loneliness as we go through life. Having time to oneself to think, dream, and create may be a lovely thing. For many of us, though, being alone may also be difficult and uncomfortable. We shall examine the power of finding solace in solitude in this chapter.

It's not necessary to completely forsake social interaction in order to find comfort in isolation. It's about realizing the importance of solitude and learning to value it. A moment of intense contemplation, recharging, and life reflection can happen while we are alone. In the absence of external interruptions, it can also be a time for creativity and free thought.

*Dilasha Adhikari*

We learn to like our own company when we develop comfort in being by ourselves. We no longer worry about being alone because we understand that we can make our own happiness. This is a crucial skill to learn since it makes us more susceptible to disappointment and hopelessness when we depend too heavily on other people or things for our happiness.

Maintaining a healthy relationship with ourselves is crucial if we want to find solace in solitude. This entails discovering how to embrace ourselves as we are, warts and all. Additionally, it entails looking after our bodily, mental, and emotional well-being.

*Dilasha Adhikari*

When we feel good about ourselves, we are better able to face the difficulties that life presents. Engaging in enjoyable hobbies is one of the best ways to get comfortable while we're by ourselves. Any activity that allows us to do this, such as reading a book, going on a walk in the countryside, or just sitting still and thinking, can be used. Finding what works for each of us and making time for it consistently is what matters.

Mindfulness is a different technique for finding comfort in solitude. Being completely present and observing things as they are without passing judgment is what mindfulness is all about. We may develop an appreciation for the beauty of the world around us and learn to be at peace in the here and now by engaging in mindfulness practices.

*Dilasha Adhikari*

Finally, the ability to find solace in isolation is a potent weapon that can aid us in coping with life's ups and downs. It involves developing a healthy relationship with oneself, partaking in things we enjoy, growing mindfulness, and getting support when we need it. It also involves learning to appreciate our own company. In your experiences of solitude, keep in mind that you are not alone. You might discover that embracing the power of solitude helps you experience greater levels of contentment, happiness, and calm.

*Dilasha Adhikari*

Don't accomplish things in Life.
Instead, Experience Life.
Be it, High or Low
Be it, Happy or Sad,
Be it, Good or Bad,
Be it, Sooner or Later,
All you should do is
EXPERIENCE IT.

*Dilasha Adhikari*

# Self-Reflection and Personal Development

Imagine a quiet lake at dawn with a glass-like surface. You may see your own reflection in the quiet of that moment as much as the lake. Self-reflection acts as a kind of soul mirror, which is what it does.

Being by yourself is like being given a lantern by life to navigate the dark passageways of your mind. It's not always simple; in fact, at times it feels like getting lost in a maze. But keep in mind that there is always a route out of a maze, and self-reflection is your compass.

*Dilasha Adhikari*

Consider yourself a canvas that life paints with experiences. Self-reflection gives you the ability to take a step back and consider the lines, tones, and patterns that have moulded you. You start to comprehend your own artistic achievement as a result of this perception.

You might want to adjust some of the brushstrokes on your painting that don't accurately represent who you are. The colours of your goals and desires are mixed on your artist's palette during self-reflection. You get to pick which ones to highlight and which to subtly fade.

*Dilasha Adhikari*

However, personal development goes beyond simply polishing your canvas and includes adding fresh layers. Consider yourself as a gardener taking care of your mental landscape. When you're alone yourself, you sow the seeds of your own growth. By creating room for fresh concepts and abilities to develop, you are nourishing the soil of your potential.

Yes, there may be moments of uncertainty, just as there are clouds that cover the sun. "Can you really change?" these doubts could mutely ask. But remember that each sunrise comes after dusk. You have to overcome your doubts and embrace your potential, which comes from self-reflection.

If you do not trust yourself, no one will either.

*Dilasha Adhikari*

Take the situation of a mountain climb. Despite the difficulty of the journey, you have a better understanding of the environment around you with each step. You can reach a greater vantage point in your life through self-reflection. It's the place where you come to terms with your weaknesses, acknowledge your strengths, and find the means to become the best version of yourself.

*Dilasha Adhikari*

So, don't be afraid to reflect on yourself when you're by yourself. It is a gift with the capacity to change you. Accept the silence, pay attention to your heart's whispers, and let self-reflection be the compass pointing you in the direction of personal development and fulfillment. As you proceed along this path, you'll come to understand that being by yourself isn't just a fleeting experience; rather, it's a canvas, a garden, and a mountain waiting for you to discover, absorb, and develop.

*Dilasha Adhikari*

We have an exceptional chance to connect with ourselves more closely when we find ourselves alone. It empowers us to simply take a step back from outside influences and concentrate on what we are feeling and thinking.

The voyage of self-discovery never entirely comes to a conclusion. Understanding our personality, our principles, and our life's goals is a journey. We're given ample opportunity and space to think about these issues without hindrance while we are by ourselves. By contemplating our past decisions, we are more aware of who we are.

*Dilasha Adhikari*

When we discover aspects about ourselves that we may not like, the journey of self-discovery can be intimidating. However, it's crucial to keep in consideration that self-discovery is about embracing who we are as an individual rather than evaluating who we are. We can begin living with greater honesty if we accept our flaws and strengths.

Self-discovery inevitably leads to personal progress. As we gain more consciousness of who we are, we have the power to change for the greater good. This may involve making new resolutions, modifying our daily patterns, or creating fresh connections. Being by oneself can provide us with the time and space to grow personally. Self-development is about being the best version possible of ourselves.

*Dilasha Adhikari*

Writing in a journal is one of the most effective ways to explore your inner self and advance personally. Clarity and perspective can be attained by putting our ideas and emotions on paper. It can be a useful tool for monitoring our development and determining areas in which we might improve.

Utilizing one's creative talents is another method of self-discovery. Painting, illustrating, or creating poetry are examples of this. We may have hidden or underutilized elements of ourselves that the creative process might help us access. Additionally, it is a potent means of facilitating emotional recovery.

*Dilasha Adhikari*

Stepping outside of our comfort zones and seeking out new experiences are equally vital. It's possible to learn new things about ourselves by attempting new things.

Additionally, it can assist us in escaping constrictive attitudes and behavioural patterns. Finally, knowledge of oneself and one's own development require endurance and compassion for oneself. It is likely that we will make errors and encounter impediments along our journey. But it's crucial that we remain mindful the fact that growth is a process, and we are all still developing. We can achieve significant personal progress by being kind to ourselves and remaining dedicated to the process.

Dilasha Adhikari

# Building meaningful relationship

The absence of a company does not imply isolation. The ability to be alone can really enable us to forge closer, more meaningful bonds with other people. This chapter will examine how being by ourselves can really improve our capacity for interpersonal connection and the development of close relationships.

**Growing a strong sense of self is the first step** in creating meaningful relationships. We are better able to connect with others when we feel at ease in our own skin and have a clear awareness of our own beliefs and priorities. The time and space aloneness affords for introspection and self-discovery can aid in the development of this sense of self.

*Dilasha Adhikari*

**The ability to communicate is another crucial aspect** in developing lasting partnerships. By giving us the chance to practise expressing ourselves and listening to others without interruptions, being alone can aid in the development of improved communication skills. During our alone time, we can also consider how we communicate and pinpoint areas that need work.

**Finding people who have similar values and interests** to our own is also crucial. We may have more time to explore our interests and hobbies while we are by ourselves, as well as to find people who have similar interests. One way to do this is by participating in clubs, going to events, or simply just talking to people who have similar interests to our own.

*Dilasha Adhikari*

Finding others who are like us is important, but it's not the only requirement for forming meaningful connections. Being receptive to learning from people with various viewpoints and experiences is another important aspect. Being alone can provide us with the time and space to consider our own prejudices and to view others objectively.

Developing compassion and empathy is another crucial component in creating meaningful connections. Our ability to connect with our emotions and comprehend those of others when we are by ourselves can aid in the development of these traits. In order to do this, one can practise mindfulness, take care of oneself, and pay attention to other people.

*Dilasha Adhikari*

**The capacity for vulnerability is the final requirement** for establishing meaningful connections. Although it can be frightening, doing this is necessary for building strong relationships with other people. It is courage, not weakness, to be vulnerable. It's about expressing who you really are, worries and all. These layers become apparent when you're by yourself. You acknowledge your dreams and face your worries. This self-awareness serves as your basis.

*Dilasha Adhikari*

When we are by ourselves, we have the time and space to examine our weaknesses and develop the confidence to reveal them to others.

Consider vulnerability now as a link to other people. It involves telling your story and hearing others.

But the truth is that sharing only happens after you've accepted your own vulnerability and you are given this room by solitude. Deep connections can be made when you're at peace with your own flaws. Vulnerability and solitude become your pillars of strength. So, when you're alone, be aware that you're getting ready for connections.

*Dilasha Adhikari*

Allow vulnerability to create ties with others when you're with them. It is a path from individual discovery to mutual comprehension.

Finally, it's important to note that being alone actually helps us form deep connections. We may create lasting relationships with others by strengthening our sense of self, developing our communication abilities, looking for like-minded people, being receptive to learning from others, developing empathy and compassion, and being willing to be vulnerable.

Dilasha Adhikari

However,

remember that creating lasting connections takes time, effort, and a willingness to take chances. Nevertheless, the benefits are great.

*Dilasha Adhikari*

Stars can shine
Brighter than
Your Future,
But,
Remember
You can be that
STAR.

Dilasha Adhikari

# How to Be Mindful When You're Alone

It's easy to become lost in our own thoughts and feelings when we're alone since it may sometimes feel overpowering. Even when we are alone, mindfulness techniques can help us stay in the present and keep us rooted in reality. We'll look at different mindfulness techniques in this chapter to see how they could help us develop a stronger sense of self-awareness.

Dilasha Adhikari

## 1) The practice of meditation

One of the greatest ways to practice mindfulness by being by oneself is meditation. It entails sitting calmly and focusing on the here and now, usually by focusing on the breath. We become more acquainted with ourselves and our innermost being. when we meditate given that we learn to analyze our thoughts and feelings objectively.

*Dilasha Adhikari*

Setting out a certain time each day to meditate, even for a short while, is one method to begin a meditation practice. Find a spot to sit that is peaceful and comfortable, and try to concentrate on your breathing. When your thoughts stray, gently refocus them on your breathing.

**2)Sense of Self**

Body awareness is yet another effective mindfulness technique for solitary meditation. This calls for becoming aware of bodily sensations, such as the sense of our feet touching the ground or the movement of our breath through our chest.

*Dilasha Adhikari*

We may refocus our attention on the present moment and develop a stronger connection with ourselves by paying attention to our bodies in this way.

Focusing on a particular body region, like your hands or feet, might help you develop body awareness. Take note of any feelings of tension, warmth, or tingling that you experience. Try to face any discomfort or suffering you experience with curiosity and non-judgment rather than trying to be insensitive towards it.

*Dilasha Adhikari*

**3)Gratitude**

Gratitude exercises are another effective mindfulness technique for solitude. Even in tiring circumstances, it entails reflecting on the blessings we have. By practising thankfulness, we can change our viewpoint and discover happiness and purpose in the here and now. Imagine sitting by a window during a rainstorm. You're all by yourself, but there's something magical in the quiet. This moment of solitude is like a treasure chest waiting to be opened. It's a chance to find the magic of gratitude, the magic of appreciating what you already have.

*Dilasha Adhikari*

Try setting out a little period of time each day to think about your many blessings as a way to cultivate appreciation. This can be accomplished by recording them in a notebook or simply thinking about them. Consider how a lovely sunset or a kind word from a friend may make us feel grateful and happy even in the smallest of things.

Consider the moments that made you laugh, learn, and grow that are among your favourite recollections. The memories you have are like priceless gems in your heart. These treasures are yours to take out and enjoy when you're by yourself. Despite all the ups and downs, you can be grateful for the journey you've been on.

*Dilasha Adhikari*

So, when you find yourself alone, take a deep breath and look around. See the simple things that often go unnoticed. Feel gratitude for the journey you've had, the people who care about you, and the small moments that make life so incredibly special.

## 4) Self-Compassion

The final mindfulness technique for being alone is to practise self-compassion. Being by ourselves makes it simple to lose ourselves in critical self-talk. However, by engaging in self-compassion exercises, we can develop the ability to treat ourselves with compassion and understanding, regardless of how we are feeling.

*Dilasha Adhikari*

You know, we often do a great job of showing kindness to other people but not as much to ourselves. You have the chance to change that in solitude. It's similar to developing a close friendship with oneself, the kind of person who encourages you when you're down and comforts you when you're sad.

To nurture self-compassion, aim to treat oneself with the same dignity and compassion that you would treat another person. When you catch yourself speaking critically toward yourself, make a conscious decision to replace it with affirmations or words of kindness.

*Dilasha Adhikari*

In the midst of everything that you do, never forget that you are deserving of love and compassion.

We can develop a deeper sense of awareness and connection with ourselves, even when we are alone ourselves, by participating in mindfulness practises. We can learn to approach ourselves and our inner world with love and understanding if we learn to incorporate daily practises like the practice of meditation, awareness of ourselves, gratitude, and empathy for ourselves.

*Dilasha Adhikari*

Consider that you are browsing through a photo album of your life. There are images of smiles, difficulties, and development. Self-compassion is like putting captions to those images that tell you you're doing your best. It's about treating oneself with the same compassion that you would have for a loved one.

It's not necessary to be flawless to be compassionate to oneself. It's about accepting your humanity, and your faults, and continuing to love yourself. It's the same as saying to yourself, "Hey, it's okay, it's not just you. You can have these discussions and provide your own consolation when you need it most in solitude.

*Dilasha Adhikari*

Imagine yourself caring for a garden. The water that supports your growth is self-compassion. You have the ability to nurture those self-love seeds when you're by yourself. That inner voice of criticism can be silenced, and its place taken with a voice of encouragement that says, "You're doing great."

*Dilasha Adhikari*

# Conquering Your Inner Demons

Imagine experiencing mental confinement every day when you awaken. You feel like you're drowning in a sea of self-doubt and anxiety due to the relentless onslaught of negative thoughts and feelings. To confront your inner demons feels like this. However, not all is bleak. In actuality, confronting your inner demons can be the beginning of a journey of self-discovery that results in empowerment and transformation. This chapter will examine strategies for overcoming your inner demons and becoming a stronger, more resilient version of yourself.

Dibasha Adhikari

**How Inner Demons Work:**

Inner demons can take on a variety of forms. They could include fear, addiction, self-doubt, worry, and sadness. They are the thoughts in your head that tell you that you are not deserving of happiness, that you are not capable of success, or that you are not good enough. They are the overwhelming feelings that make you feel powerless and isolated.

*Dilasha Adhikari*

**The Value of Confronting Your Inner Demons:**

It's like living in a jail you made for yourself if you ignore your inner demons. You feel unable to alter your circumstances and become a victim of your own bad ideas and feelings. But things don't have to be this way. You regain control of your life by embracing your inner demons. You start living life on your terms once you stop allowing your thoughts and feelings to rule you.

*Dilasha Adhikari*

# How, to Deal with Your Inner Demons:

**Recognize Your Demons:**

Recognizing your inner demons is the first step towards overcoming them. To address your concerns and doubts requires guts, yet doing so is the only way to advance.

Your thoughts are not always accurate, therefore challenge them. They frequently stem from bad experiences in the past or negative self-talk. You can reframe your thoughts in a more constructive way by challenging them. You can persuade yourself that you are competent for achievement, that you deserve love, and that you are sufficient.

*Dilasha Adhikari*

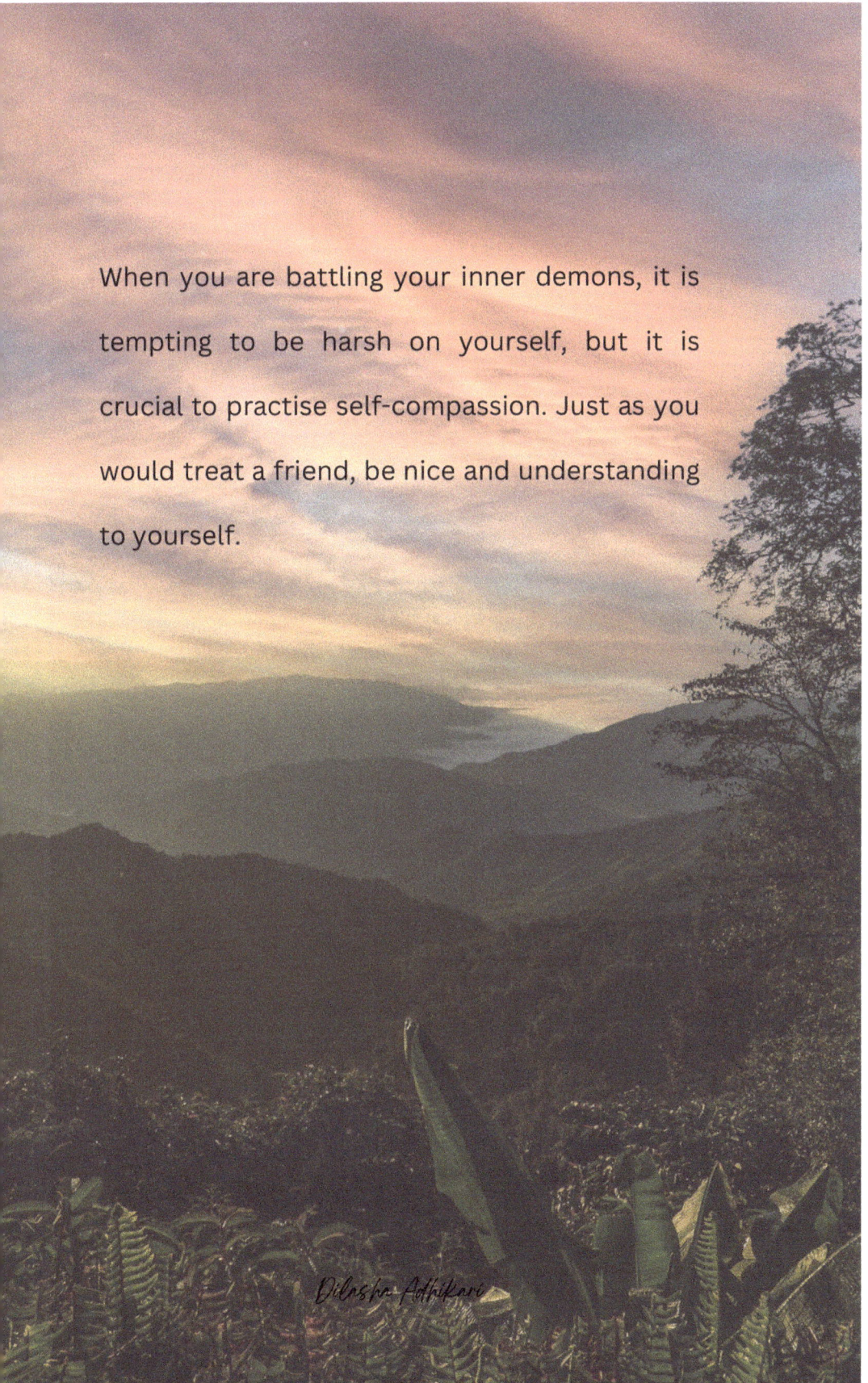

When you are battling your inner demons, it is tempting to be harsh on yourself, but it is crucial to practise self-compassion. Just as you would treat a friend, be nice and understanding to yourself.

*Dilasha Adhikari*

# Learnings from Confronting Your Inner Demons:

**You Can Overcome Your Inner Demons**: When you face your inner demons, you realize that you are stronger than you believe. Unbeknown to you, you possess strength and fortitude.

**Failure Is Not the End:** You will stumble and fall as you confront your inner demons. Failure does not spell doom, though. It's a chance for you to develop, learn, grow, and improve. There is no Failure in life, there is only experience and where there is experience, there is learning.

*Dilasha Adhikari*

**You are not Alone:** There are actually numerous others who wrestle with inner demons besides you. Everyone has them. You become conscious of the fact that you're part of an even larger community when you express your difficulties to others. You receive assistance, compassion, and comprehension.

It takes guts and tenacity to confront your inner demons on your quest for self-discovery. While not an easy path, it is one that should be pursued. You become a more resilient and powerful version of yourself as you vanquish your inner demons. As soon as you regain control over your life, you may begin living the life you were destined to lead.

*Dilasha Adhikari*

In the World.
Where everyone is racing to be like someone else,
You be the best version of Yourself.

*Dilasha Adhikari*

# Embracing Creativity and Imagination – The Pathway to Self-Expression

Do you still have vivid memories of the happiness and excitement you felt as a young child when you were making art, constructing forts, and conjuring wonderful worlds? Many of us lose touch with our creative side as we get older and start prioritizing practicality above inspiration. A fulfilling existence, however, depends on embracing imagination and creativity. We'll look at the advantages of encouraging imagination and creativity, as well as how doing so can promote self-expression and personal development, in this chapter.

*Dilasha Adhikari*

# The Influence of Imagination and Creativity:

Not only are artists and writers capable of creativity and imagination. We may utilize them as instruments to express ourselves, find solutions, and develop. Our creative side opens up a world of opportunities for us. We develop greater adaptability, curiosity, and openness. We develop the ability to view things from several angles and come up with fresh solutions to problems.

*Dilasha Adhikari*

# Having a strong sense of self is important:

Sharing one's thoughts, emotions, and ideas with others is a kind of self-expression. In order to interact and communicate with others, it is crucial.

By being authentic, we urge people to connect with us more deeply. Do you remember how we connect to certain people instantly? It's because they were so authentic and were interacting with us from their soul. It's their soul connecting to ours, as in the end, we all are a spirit in the human body.

This is possible when we express ourselves. Additionally, self-expression can support our emotional processing and aid in overcoming adversity.

*Dilasha Adhikari*

# How to Encourage Creativity and Imagination:

**Find Time for Play:** Everyone can enjoy themselves. Adults must have it as well. Make time in your daily schedule to do things that make you happy and let you express your creativity. This could be in written form, the act of dancing, or any other means of self-expression.

***Try New Things:*** Pushing yourself beyond what is familiar might be nerve-wracking, but it's actually a fantastic way to unlock your imagination and creativity. Take up a new pastime, explore an unfamiliar place, or enrol in a class about a subject you are passionate about.

*Dilasha Adhikari*

**Use mindfulness to your advantage:** Mindfulness is the art of being in the present. We are more conscious of our surroundings, and thoughts when we are mindful. Our creative side can be tapped and inspiration can be found in our everyday lives with the aid of this understanding.

**Join Forces with Others:** Joining forces with other people is a fantastic method to unleash your imagination and creativity. Being a part of a team could assist you in seeing things from different angles and bringing fresh ideas to the table.

Now let's provoke your thoughts with this question;

*When you close your eyes and dream, what kind of world are you creating within yourself?*

*Dilasha Adhikari*

# Lessons For Life from Using Imagination and Creativity

**You Are Unique:**

Whenever you value your imagination and creativity, you come to understand that you have something special to contribute to the world. Your ideas and thoughts are valuable, and you should express them.

**You Will Fail When You Create:**

it's part of the process. Every concept won't be a genius one. The process, however, includes failure. It presents an opportunity for skill improvement, learning, and growth. Remember what I said earlier, failure is an experience to come up with an improvement.

Failing is not the end of the world, it gives you an opportunity to start all over again but with experience.

*Dilasha Adhikari*

## Self-expression Is Empowering:

Because it allows you to take control of your feelings and thoughts. You gain self-assurance and strength as a result, and you allow others to experience the same thing.

Living a fulfilling life requires embracing creativity and imagination.

A whole new world of opportunities becomes available when we exercise our creative side.

We develop greater adaptability, curiosity, and openness. We develop the ability to view things from several angles and come up with fresh solutions to problems.

By expressing ourselves, we encourage stronger connections with people and build our self-assurance and power. So go ahead and use your imagination and creativity; explore wherever it leads you.

*Dilasha Adhikari*

We develop greater adaptability, curiosity, and openness. We develop the ability to view things from several angles and come up with fresh solutions to problems.

By expressing ourselves, we encourage stronger connections with people and build our self-assurance and power. So go ahead and use your imagination and creativity; explore wherever it leads you.

*Dilasha Adhikari*

Be gentle with Yourself as you Heal. You're doing the best you can.

*Dilasha Adhikari*

# Cultivating Gratitude and Appreciation – The Key to Unlocking Happiness

Ever notice how simple it is to concentrate on your life's problems? We frequently lose sight of the many benefits and joys all around us as a result of our propensity to focus only on our difficulties and hardships. A world of enjoyment and fulfilment can be unlocked by practising thankfulness and appreciation, which can help us turn our attention inward. The advantages of developing thankfulness and appreciation, as well as how they might change our lives, are discussed in this chapter.

*Dilasha Adhikari*

**The Influence of Appreciation and Gratitude:**

Positive emotions are drawn to expressions of gratitude and admiration. We draw a greater quantity of the same things into our lives when we concentrate on what we have to be thankful for. We start to appreciate the little blessings we have every day, which makes us happier and more pleased. Also significantly affecting our relationships are feelings of gratitude and admiration. We enhance our relationships and establish trust when we show others how much we appreciate them.

*Dilasha Adhikari*

## The Value of Attitude

Our capacity to develop thankfulness and appreciation is greatly influenced by our mentality. It's simple to ignore the positive aspects of our lives and concentrate on the negative when we have a pessimistic perspective. However, when we adopt an attitude of thankfulness and admiration, we start to perceive the world around us in a different way. We discover joy in the little things as we grow more conscious of the many benefits in our lives.

*Dilasha Adhikari*

# How to Develop Gratitude and Appreciation

**1) Keep a gratitude journal every day:**

spend a few minutes listing a few things for which you are thankful. A beautiful day, a thoughtful act from a friend, or a satisfying lunch are just a few examples of what this might be.

**2) Use mindfulness to your advantage:** Mindfulness is the art of being in the present. By practising mindfulness, we raise our level of consciousness regarding our thoughts and feelings and learn to value even the little things in life.

*Dilasha Adhikari*

**3) Take the time to let loved ones know how much you appreciate them.** Saying "thank you" or penning a sincere note could be all that is required.

**4) Try to concentrate on the positive parts of your life** rather than dwelling on your issues. Your work, relationships, or overall health may be at stake.

*Dilasha Adhikari*

# Lessons for Life from Developing Gratitude and Appreciation:

1) **We have the ability to select our attitude and to concentrate on the positive aspects of our existence.** We can access a whole universe of happiness and fulfilment when we practise gratitude and appreciation.

2) **Appreciation is the Foundation of Relationships.** When we show others how much we value them, we fortify our bonds and establish trust. Effective and productive relationships necessitate appreciation.

*Dilasha Adhikari*

**3)Being Thankful Is the Cure for Negativity.** We invite more happiness into our lives when we concentrate on our blessings. Positive thinking is treated with gratitude.

Therefore,

The secret to happiness and fulfilment in our lives lies in cultivating gratitude and appreciation. We start to perceive the world differently when we change our perspective to one of gratitude and appreciation.

*Dilasha Adhikari*

We discover joy in the little things as we grow more conscious of the many benefits in our lives. By expressing our gratitude to others, we also deepen our connections and create a sense of trust. In order to increase your happiness and fulfillment, take a few minutes each day to concentrate on the positive aspects of your life and remember along the way you can not make everyone happy either.

Everyone will hurt you at one point in your life, don't depend on others for your peace and happiness because your life is your responsibility.

*Dilasha Adhikari*

# Lessons for Life from Including Alone Time:

- When we give ourselves time to unwind we provide ourselves with the opportunity to think about and engage with our true selves. A greater sense of clarity and self-awareness may result from this.

- Taking time for oneself is not selfish; rather, it is an essential component of self-care. We are better equipped to be there for those around us in our lives when we put our needs first.

- For creativity, alone time is essential. The greatest philosophers and artists in history frequently worked alone. Finding new inspiration and ideas can be facilitated by solitude.

*Dilasha Adhikari*

Hence, For our psychological and emotional welfare, it is imperative that we build time for ourselves into our daily schedules. We give ourselves time to think, rest, and reconnect with our true selves whenever we spend time for ourselves. higher clarity, less tension, and a higher feeling of self-awareness can result from this.

Setting boundaries, being clear about what we need from those in our lives, and prioritizing time for ourselves as a kind of self-care are all crucial. Therefore, set aside sometime each day to tune out the outside world and concentrate on yourself. The tranquillity and clarity you discover can astound you.

*Dilasha Adhikari*

# Understanding Yourself

Think of a library full of books, each one containing a tale. Imagine yourself as one of those unread books right now. It's like opening a book and reading your own story when you're all alone. It's an inside voyage, an introspective journey. You may get the chance to explore the deepest parts of who you are when you find yourself all alone. Introspection, a method of self-examination that enables you to examine your deepest ideas and emotions, is the first step on this journey. You can better grasp who you are, your goals, and your motivations by engaging in introspection.

The art of introspection involves searching within yourself for answers to your deepest questions, much like searching for buried treasure.

*Dilasha Adhikari*

Sometimes life moves quickly, like a river, and we are too preoccupied to pause and observe our own reflection. Your calm pond is solitude. When you drop a pebble of self-awareness, introspection is the ripples that appear. It involves gaining a clearer perspective on yourself and recognizing both your accomplishments and your room for improvement.

Self-analysis is an essential part of this procedure. It necessitates that you stop what you're doing in the middle of your daily tasks and take a moment to consider your ideas, feelings, and experiences. You can accomplish this by journaling, practising meditation, or just going on a long walk by yourself in the wilderness.

*Dilasha Adhikari*

You can start to investigate your values and beliefs through this self-reflection. What do you believe in? What tenets govern your life? What and why do you adhere to? Though they can be challenging to respond to, these questions are crucial for forging a solid sense of self.

You will learn about your talents and shortcomings as you continue on this trip. What do you excel at? What do you find challenging? You may create attainable objectives and make prudent choices about your life by being aware of your talents and weaknesses.

*Dilasha Adhikari*

Finally, knowing oneself requires having a strong sense of self. This entails being aware of what you are thinking, feeling, and doing right now. It entails embracing yourself as you are, with all your imperfections, and actively working to become a better version of yourself.

In other words, the path to self-discovery begins with understanding oneself. It necessitates a close examination of your identity, your values, and your life goals. Though emotionally taxing and difficult at times, the journey is definitely worth the effort.

You may start living a life that is genuine, rewarding, and authentic to who you are by developing a keen sense of self-awareness.

*Dilasha Adhikari*

# Discovering Your Passion

When we are alone, we may have the chance to explore passions and interests that we may not have had the time or space to do so in the past. Without the interruptions and expectations of others, being alone enables us to listen to our inner voice. It may be an appropriate opportunity to consider what genuinely makes us happy and fulfilled.

t's crucial to get involved in pursuits that pique our attention and curiosity in order to find our passions. This can entail picking up a new hobby, reading a book, or taking in the outdoors.

*Dilasha Adhikari*

We are more likely to find new passions that we might have otherwise neglected when we participate in enjoyable activities.

Finding our hobbies may be a very emotional process. It might evoke emotions of doubt and apprehension along with sensations of delight, excitement, and curiosity. It is crucial that we embrace this endeavour with a mind and heart that are open, allowing ourselves to feel all of the feelings that surface.

Once we've identified our passions, it's critical to actively pursue them. Setting objectives and pursuing them entails pushing through difficulties or overwhelming circumstances.

*Dilasha Adhikari*

By giving us a feeling of meaning and purpose in life, pursuing our interests may be a highly effective source of encouragement and fulfilment.

Finding our passions ultimately involves a journey that takes time, patience, and introspection. It may be a life-changing event that inspires us to lead a more genuine and satisfying existence. We can uncover new facets of who we are and realize our full potential by viewing being alone as a possibility to pursue our passions.

*Dilasha Adhikari*

Do not forget that your secret ingredient is your passion. It is the component that has the power to transform a routine day into a noteworthy one. Start your voyage now, be open to the unknown, and let your passion be the compass that guides you to a world of adventure and discovery. Who knows? You might simply stumble across a secret ability or a previously unknown level of happiness!

In Solitude find
your light,
learning to cherish
Yourself day and
Night,
Embrace scars that
once brought pain,
slowly in self-
love,
you will attain.

*Dilasha Adhikari*

# Setting Goals And Taking Action

In order to reach our potential and live a satisfying life, setting objectives is essential. Setting realistic goals, though, can be difficult. It's crucial to tackle this process deliberately and clearly.

The ability to visualize is a strong tool for reaching our objectives. When we visualize our objectives, we can clearly see what we want to accomplish and how it will make us feel once we have them. When faced with challenges and setbacks, this keeps us inspired and determined.

*Dilasha Adhikari*

It can be difficult to set goals and take action, but the strength of solitude can make it simpler. Spending time alone can help you gain the clarity and focus you need to decide what matters most to you and create goals that are in line with your beliefs and aspirations.

Think about your goals and why they are important to you while you are alone yourself. Exploring your deepest wants and aspirations can be an emotional process. Make a plan to complete each of your goals one at a time by breaking them down into manageable, smaller steps. Give each task a fixed end date and be clear about what you aim to achieve.

*Dilasha Adhikari*

It can be emotionally taxing to take steps toward your goals. It can be intimidating to venture outside of what you're used to and attempt new activities, but always remember to start small and progress steadily. You'll gain momentum and remain inspired to move forward as a result.

Refrain from being too hard on yourself when you run into challenges or failures. Consider what went wrong during your alone time and make the necessary changes to your strategy. Achieving your goals requires being adaptable and flexible, therefore don't be hesitant to change course when necessary.

*Dilasha Adhikari*

# Understanding the value of personal space in a relationship (Finding room to Breathe)

There are times when all we need is a little breathing room, and we've all had those experiences. It's not that we don't care about or love the people in our life; rather, there are moments when we long for some alone time to rest, think, and just be. Here, respect for personal space is important.

Personal space is like a comfortable corner that is all yours. You can withdraw there and re-establish contact with your own ideas, feelings, and dreams. It's about striking a good balance between togetherness and individuality, not about alienating others.

*Dilasha Adhikari*

Personal space is essential in all types of relationships, including romantic, familial, and friendship ones. We are able to keep our freedom and feelings of self. We develop more contented personalities when we have the freedom to pursue our own interests, partake in pastimes that make us happy, and have time to ourselves. Nevertheless, when we are content, we bring a more powerful and genuine version of ourselves to our interactions with others.

Personal space does not imply separation or disconnection from our loved ones. Actually, it's the complete opposite. Respecting our desire for personal space allows us to foster happier, better connections with others.

*Dilasha Adhikari*

It enables us to come across as our best selves, with fresh vigour, love, and admiration.

Now visualize a lovely garden where flowers are permitted to develop freely. Even though each flower blooms in a different way, they all coexist and enhance and complement one another's beauty. Similar to those flowers, personal space in relationships enables us to grow personally while fostering our connection with others.

How then do we strike this fine balance between proximity and private time? The key is communication.

*Dilasha Adhikari*

Encourage your loved ones to voice their own needs for privacy by being transparent with them about your need for alone time. You foster a climate of trust and support by being aware of and respecting each other's boundaries.

Personal space is ultimately a priceless gift we may provide to ourselves and our loved ones. It serves as a reminder that even though we are each on our own distinct journeys, we still decide to share some aspects of our lives with others. By respecting personal space, we take care of our own well-being and foster closer, more satisfying bonds with others.

So, choose your favourite hiding place, take a moment to breathe, and see how your connections can become more beautiful when you have a private space.

*Dilasha Adhikari*

# Solitude: A Sanctuary for Healing and Self-Care

Ever found comfort in being alone with your thoughts during a peaceful period? when your environment becomes less noticeable and you can, at last, hear the murmurs of your own heart? These are quiet times, and they have great power for healing and taking care of oneself.

We frequently overlook taking care of ourselves in our busy lives. We lose ourselves in the never-ending demands and expectations, ignoring the most crucial person in our lives: ourselves. However, we can find solace, healing, and a subtly affirming reminder of our importance within the embrace of solitude.

*Dilasha Adhikari*

We are given a priceless chance in solitude to reconnect with our inner selves and to remove the tension and commotion from our environment. It's a hallowed place where we may shed our masks and embrace our frailties without fear of criticism. We can really start the healing and self-care path inside this sanctuary. We make room to hear our own needs and desires when we give ourselves permission to be alone. We might consider the events of the past, acknowledge our suffering, and attempt to mend the internal wounds that remain open. We are given the time and space by solitude to care for our emotional health and to compassionately mend the holes in our hearts.

*Dilasha Adhikari*

We find our own special routes to self-care in the quiet stillness.

Even though face masks and bubble baths can be relaxing, self-care is more than that. It involves taking care of our overall health and nurturing our mind, body, and soul.

Solitude offers us the blank canvas on which to create our masterpiece of self-care.

It's crucial to recognize that it won't always be simple when we start this journey of healing and self-care. There may be times when the stillness is unsettling when old wounds reopen, and when the weight of our emotions seems too much to carry.

But in these times, solitude stands by our side, comforting us and reassuring us that we have what it takes to overcome.

*Dilasha Adhikari*

I implore you to seek out the embrace of solitude if you find yourself yearning for comfort or a brief moment of calm amidst the craziness of life. Make time in your schedule for periods of solitude, reflection, and self-care. Your well-being depends on it, and you deserve it. On this profound journey of healing and self-care, accept isolation as your refuge, your gentle healer, and your steadfast guide.

*Dilasha Adhikari*

# Overcoming trauma and finding solace in solitary moments

**Trigger Warning: In this chapter, we will discuss sensitive topics related to trauma. Please ensure you are in a safe and supportive space before proceeding.**

We all carry the traces of our past at the very core of who we are. Some events leave deep psychological scars that influence our ideas, feelings, and perceptions. Trauma can have a lasting impact on our lives in a variety of ways. However, there is also the opportunity for tremendous healing and transformation amid the shadows.

*Dilasha Adhikari*

It takes a lot of courage, openness, and self-compassion to overcome trauma. Everyone follows a different route because the wounds we bear are as individual as fingerprints. But in recognizing that we are not alone in our challenges, we can find comfort and support in our shared humanity.

Think of yourself as an adventurous traveller negotiating the difficult terrain of your own experiences. In order to overcome trauma, you must sow seeds of hope in the soil of your suffering. It's about rewriting your story and transforming the hurtful chapters into healing ones.

*Dilasha Adhikari*

Imagine yourself in a room with nothing but the gentle cocoon of stillness around you. It's just you and your thoughts, conversing like long-lost friends around a roaring fire. It is lonely here. You can let your thoughts float here without anyone judging you; only understanding.

These quiet times develop into a kind of spiritual shelter for you as you move through your healing process. A place to cradle your grief and turn it into resilience, it's where you go aside from the commotion to sit with your emotions.

.

*Dilasha Adhikari*

Keep in mind that recovering from trauma is similar to a tree growing steadily and slowly after a storm. And those quiet times are like the sun that feeds your growth and the rain that wipes away the hurt. Take advantage of these times because they are reminders of your courage, resiliency, and capacity to recover and emerge even stronger than before.

Trauma can make us feel as though our fundamental foundation has been shaken. We might experience overwhelming emotions, haunting memories, or a sense of disconnection from the outside world. The suffering can be oppressive, making us doubt our value, our purpose, and our capacity to ever experience happiness once more.

*Dilasha Adhikari*

Trauma leaves its mark like a hurricane. It's acceptable to have those scars, but it's also crucial to take care of them. Your haven of safety and protection becomes solitude, where you can tenderly cradle your scars and reassure them that you recognize and see them.

Think of yourself as the owner of a priceless vase that has been broken. The best time to repair such cracks is in solitude, one at a time. Applying the salve of self-care to each unpleasant memory is the goal. It serves as a reminder that recovery is a process that requires time rather than race.

Remember that healing involves changing your relationship with the past, not eliminating it. You have a blank canvas in solitude on which to paint your own story and rework it with resiliency and compassion for yourself. It's an opportunity to affirm, "I endured, and I will prosper."

*Dilasha Adhikari*

You can heal, I just want you to know that. The tenacity and adaptability of the human spirit are astounding. The wounds need not define us, even though they could still be present. As a result, they serve as a symbol of our resilience and capacity to overcome challenges.

We must first accept the suffering and its effects on our lives before we can start the healing process. To face the memories and emotions we have buried deep within ourselves, to face the darkness within, requires tremendous courage. But by bringing attention to our suffering, we can start to break its hold on our emotions. As we work to recover from trauma, we may find hidden dimensions of who we are—seeds, of empathy, compassion, and fortitude that sprout in the face of hardship. In addition to changing our lives, healing allows us to become rays of hope and inspiration for others who may be going through the same thing.

*Dilasha Adhikari*

# Seeking Solitude in a Digital World

Solitude has turned into a valuable item in the middle of this fast-paced, digital world we live in—a hidden jewel that we long for but struggle to achieve. Technology has ingrained itself into every aspect of our lives, and we are continually barraged with alerts, messages, and a never-ending flood of information. Visualize entering a busy metropolis where screens, sounds, and a wealth of information are all around you. The digital world is like this bustling city—it never sleeps. There is, however, a quiet area waiting for you in the middle of this digital pandemonium, like a secret garden where you can catch your breath. In this chapter, we set out on a moving quest to rediscover the value of isolation in a society that places a premium on continual communication.

*Dilasha Adhikari*

We find ourselves at a fork in the road as we wade through the waves of constant connectivity. On the one hand, technology has enabled us to communicate with people around the world and has provided us with great convenience. The way we work, study and communicate has been completely transformed. On the other hand, though, it has also hurt our capacity to find comfort within ourselves.

The constant notification buzzing, the allure of continuous scrolling, and the anxiety over missing out on other people's virtual lives have made us prisoners.

*Dilasha Adhikari*

We have lost the skill of spending time in quiet solitude with our thoughts and enjoying our own company. The idea of solitude has lost all of its meaning; it is now something we long for.

You can rediscover what is authentic while you are alone, both offline and online. In order to connect with people more deeply, it's important to see past filters and emojis. In a world where most interactions are on the surface, it's like having in-depth discussions with people.

However, we must acknowledge the deep effects of solitude on our health in the middle of this digital turmoil. We may actually hear our own soul's whispers, rediscover our passions, and connect with our most enduring desires when we are alone. Instead of being a burden, solitude can be a place where we can nurture our inner selves and discover clarity in the middle of chaos.

*Dilasha Adhikari*

We must first master healthy limits and effective technology management if we are to recover the power of solitude. It's time to regain control and establish sacred areas in our lives where we can disconnect and re-establish contact with our own thoughts and feelings.

To set boundaries with our technologies, we must make a purposeful, conscious effort. Turning off notifications that continuously disturb our peace and divert our focus is a good place to start. A kitchen table where meals are enjoyed without devices, or a quiet corner where we can curl up with a book rather than continually scrolling through social media feeds, are just a few examples of places in our homes that we might designate as device-free zones.

*Dilasha Adhikari*

Limiting our use of technology also entails restraining ourselves from compulsively grabbing our phones at every available opportunity. We might choose to cherish those quiet times instead and give ourselves permission to daydream, let our thoughts roam, and just be. Inspiration frequently occurs in these times when it seems like nothing is getting done, and the seeds of creativity start to sprout.

Keep in mind that finding isolation doesn't need you to vanish from the online world. It involves establishing areas of calm during the digital storm.

Dilashn Adhikari

We can pause and ask ourselves, "Is this bringing me joy or adding value to my life?" before mindlessly browsing through social media or slithering into a whirlwind of emails. We can reduce distractions and make room for solitude to flourish by being deliberate about how we interact with technology.

Never forget your quiet retreat when the digital metropolis becomes too much. Spend some time disconnecting, thinking, and connecting with yourself. You'll learn via these digital breaks that solitude isn't lost in the digital jungle; rather, it's a guiding star that pulls you back to your authentic self even when surrounded by screens and pixels.

*Dilasha Adhikari*

# Exploring the connection between solitude and spirituality

The relationship between solitude and spirituality is something I want to briefly discuss with you. It's a subject that touches the core of who we are and where we belong in this great universe, and it makes us feel deeply.

Your sanctuary of peace in a world that is constantly moving is solitude. It's like discovering a place of worship where you can have a spiritual experience, where the noise of the outside world disappears and just your soul's whisper remains.

*Dilasha Adhikari*

Think of your inner spirituality as well. You raise the streams of wisdom and understanding by lowering a bucket of solitude. It offers you the chance to consider your convictions, pay attention to the reflections of your innermost thoughts, and deepen your relationship with the universe.

We embark on a spiritual journey—one that takes us to the very centre of who we are—when we are alone when we turn inward and remove ourselves from the chaos of the outside world. We make a profound connection to something bigger than ourselves here, in the gentle acceptance of solitude.

*Dilasha Adhikari*

You aren't simply alone when you are in isolation; you are also with your spiritual self. It's a moment for reflection, prayer, or just being. It's like lighting a candle in the dark, allowing your faith to show through, and having that light guide you through times of difficulty.

In order to embrace the sacred in daily life, one must keep in mind that spirituality is not about following strict procedures. Your interactions with others, your thoughts, and your acts can all be infused with spirituality when you are alone. Through the darkest times, it's like having a lantern of faith to hold.

*Dilasha Adhikari*

Ever get the sense that something is missing from your life, a deep need, an ache within your soul? Your spirit is encouraging you to look for comfort and direction in the heavenly sphere, and I think that longing is its whisper. We can respond to that appeal best in solitude.

By accepting isolation, we build a sacred container—a vessel—that enables us to access our inner spiritual source. Here we find comfort, direction, and a profound sense of connection to something that goes beyond our physical existence. We become aware of our close interconnection with the cosmos when we are alone rather than when we are with others.

By spending time alone, we can strip away the societal pressures and masks we wear and show the divine our actual selves.

*Dilasha Adhikari*

We become more open to spiritual development, change, and a strengthening of our ties to the sacred when we are vulnerable. We can let life flow through us when we are alone and believe that a greater power is directing our steps.

Solitude creates the ideal environment for spiritual encounters to take place, whether through meditation, prayer, or just being in nature.

When you are alone, you are not simply looking for solutions; you are also discovering important questions. It is similar to staring at the stars and pondering your place in the universe. It's a time for introspection, accepting life's mysteries, and seeking solace in the unknowable.

*Dilasha Adhikari*

Accept isolation as your sacred friend when you feel the pull of something larger or the universe's whisper. Spend some time being quiet, paying attention, and connecting with your spiritual core. You'll discover that solitude transforms during these peaceful times into the entranceway to a more profound spiritual connection, enhancing your journey through life with meaning, peace, and profound knowledge.

On this journey, remember that you are not travelling alone.

Find comfort in the idea that we are all connected and that we are all a part of a larger cosmic dance, and embrace the unity that lies within our shared humanity.

*Dilasha Adhikari*

May your exploration of solitude and spirituality kindle a fire within you that illuminates your way, stokes your interests, and radiates love and compassion to everyone you come in contact with.

Embrace the healing power of isolation, my friend, and allow it to lead you to a profound realization of your own divinity.

Take moments to close your eyes, open your soul, and commune with the universe.

*Dilasha Adhikari*

# Tips for incorporating solitude into daily life

Finding moments of isolation might be difficult in the chaos of our everyday life. But do not worry, I have some easy suggestions to assist you in incorporating the power of solitude into your daily activities.

**Morning Moments:**

Schedule some quiet time for yourself to start your day. You can find a quiet place to sit, breathe deeply, and let the silence wash over you. Enjoy the calm and quiet before the rest of the world awakens, or use this time to ponder or make your intentions for the day.

*Dilasha Adhikari*

**Tech Timeout:**

Give yourself a break from the nonstop hum of technology with a tech timeout. Designate certain times of the day to disconnect from your devices and unplug them. Take advantage of this time to do things you enjoy and that help you be in the present. It could be anything from daydreaming to taking a walk or reading a book.

**The Embrace of Nature:**

Nature has a way of soothing our brains and nourishing our spirits. Whether it's a weekend walk or a lunchtime visit to a neighbouring park, find time to spend in nature. Deepen your breath, feel the ground beneath your feet, and allow the natural world's magnificence to uplift your spirit.

*Dilasha Adhikari*

**Mindful Mealtimes:**

Making mealtimes attentive and nourishing is possible by adopting this strategy. Make sure to savour each piece of food rather than hurry through meals. The tastes, textures, and aromas of your food should be appreciated. Take advantage of the chance to refocus on the basic pleasures of eating and avoid outside distractions.

**Solo Strolls:** Make time to go for solitary strolls, even if they are simply around the neighbourhood. As you explore your surroundings and take in the sound of your own footsteps, let your feet lead the way. It's an opportunity to unwind, breathe in some fresh air, and relish the quiet of your own company.

*Dilasha Adhikari*

**Creative Expression:** Get creative in ways that make you happy and let you express yourself. Drawing, colouring, playing an instrument, or keeping a journal are all examples of creative expression. Enjoy the creative process and let your imagination soar as you produce something wholly original.

**Evening Unwind:** Make up a relaxing bedtime routine before going to sleep to help you relax and be ready for a sound sleep. Take some time to think about your day, read a book, enjoy a cup of tea or just relax with some music. Allow yourself to put all of your cares and tension aside and enjoy the peace of the night.

The smallest moments can contain solitude, which doesn't always involve making a big show of it. Adopt these suggestions and discover what functions the finest for you. Solace in isolation can bring you periods of introspection, tranquillity, and self-discovery. Make solitude a soothing partner in your daily life.

*Dilasha Adhikari*

# The profound impact of solitude and its lasting benefits

In a society where noise and distraction are constants, isolation provides us with a sacred haven—a place where we can withdraw and re-establish contact with our most fundamental selves. We can freely explore the vast landscapes of our thoughts, emotions, and wants while we are alone, which allows us to better understand the intricate workings of our being.

*Dilasha Adhikari*

In this stillness, we find a source of inspiration and creativity that awakens fresh insights into problems that lie dormant in the bustle of daily life. We can express our actual selves in solitude by letting go of societal expectations and accepting who we really are. Here, we discover the strength of independence and self-reliance, building resilience and self-assurance as we travel the vast territory of solitary.

We discover strength and authenticity when we reveal the layers of our vulnerability, building a path that is in line with our core beliefs and desires. When we are alone, we are able to let go of the pressure of receiving approval from others and fully engross ourselves in the rich tapestry of our own lives.

*Dilasha Adhikari*

The permanent effects of isolation that reverberate throughout our lives and change us into creatures of depth, purpose, and steadfast self-belief are only truly discovered in the quiet moments, far from the madding crowd. By acknowledging solitude, we set out on a journey that transforms us forever and motivates others to open up to their own inner worlds and discover the beauty and strength of being by themselves.

*Dilasha Adhikari*

In this world where Humans think
they are greatest of all.
They often forget there is a more
powerful force holding you all.
The creator knows about his
creation,
You are not forgotten,
Trust the Process and move on,
Because the creator can see
and hear,
which you can not do
with your eyes and ears.

*Dilasha Adhikari*

# Spirituality and Solitude: Deepening Your Connection with Universe.

Isn't there something absolutely lovely about being alone? We frequently find a profound connection to something larger than ourselves during those times when we are by ourselves with our thoughts and feelings. We can strengthen our spiritual ties to the universe while we are completely alone. When we accept isolation, we allow ourselves the chance to investigate the secrets that lay within and to dive into the depths of our souls.

*Dilasha Adhikari*

We may actually connect with the universe and feel a great sense of oneness in this hallowed location.

We cultivate a favourable environment for spiritual development and enlightenment when we quiet our brains and open our hearts.

**Imagine this:** You discover yourself in a quiet setting during the calming sounds of nature. Your spirit is soothed into a state of stillness by the symphony of sounds created by the rustling of leaves, the soft caress of the wind, and the far-off melodies of birds. You close your eyes, take a few deliberate, deep breaths, and let your mind drift away in this peaceful environment.

*Dilasha Adhikari*

You start to feel more connected as you withdraw more into this seclusion. You sense a deep connection to all living things and an awareness that you are a vital component of something far bigger than yourself. The walls that used to divide you from the world around you start to fall away, and you suddenly realize how intricately woven the fabric of existence is.

You might feel more intuitive and inner-knowing during this period of spiritual connection. The cosmos communicates with you through nudges and symbols, directing you on your path to self-awareness and development. You can discover that you're drawn to certain writings, ideas, or practices that speak to your soul and teach you things you didn't know existed.

*Dilasha Adhikari*

The road to spirituality is a very individual one. Your soul's resonance may be distinct from other people's resonance. Accept this distinction and give yourself permission to define and pursue your own spiritual path. Let your heart be your guide and trust your intuition.

*Dilasha Adhikari*

# Overcoming Social Pressure: Embracing Your Authentic Self

I have a feeling that you are bearing the weight of the world and the pressure of societal expectations. I can't help but feel heartbroken as I feel you struggle to find your way through the social pressure minefield. But pay close attention because you possess an unbreakable spirit and a bright light that longs to be released and reveal the way to your true self.

The messages of who we should be, how we should seem, and what we should accomplish are continually being thrown at us in the world in which we live.

*Dilasha Adhikari*

It can be exhausting to be under so much pressure to fit in and follow social norms. It speaks to you in a whisper, telling you to cover your individuality and stifle your inner identity.

I am aware that the road to honesty can be difficult and fraught with doubt and anxiety. To emerge from the darkness of social norms and into the brightness of your true identity takes courage. But keep in mind that you are not defined by the views of others. The only approval you really need is the one that originates from your own heart.

For a moment, close your eyes and picture a world free from cultural influences. Your interests, eccentricities, and dreams are embraced here rather than mocked.

*Dilasha Adhikari*

Success in this life isn't determined by outward accomplishments, but rather by the degree of fulfillment and connection with your inner self. Now hold on to this image, because it offers a glimpse of the world you can choose for yourself. Start by removing the constraints that society has placed on you if you want to overcome societal pressure.

Independent of the expectations of others, consider the principles and ideals that speak to your soul. No matter how unusual they may seem, embrace the special passions, skills, and hobbies that only you possess.

You will discover a deep sense of belonging and purpose in these times of self-expression.

*Dilasha Adhikari*

Never forget, that accepting who you truly are takes work. Self-discovery and progress are a lifetime adventure. There will be times when you doubt yourself and encounter obstacles; remember to be kind and patient with yourself. But as you move forward, you'll get stronger, more confident, and more in touch with your genuine self.

You have the ability to separate yourself from the bonds of social pressure and lead an authentic life. Accept your openness as a badge of honour and a demonstration of your fortitude and resiliency. Your distinct voice, genuine presence, and true self are what the world needs.

*Dilasha Adhikari*

# The Power of Silence

There is a great force concealed in the sweet embrace of stillness, hidden among the world's confusion and continual commotion. We are able to access a source of power, discernment, and inner calm in these quiet moments.

I want to tell you about how silence has a transforming power and can help us access a strength that is greater than words.

More than just the lack of music, silence offers us a place to stop, think, and re-establish contact with our most fundamental selves. It provides a haven from the everyday barrage of external stimuli and the incessant chatter of our thoughts. We discover a hallowed place in stillness where our minds may unwind and our souls can refuel.

*Dilasha Adhikari*

We experience the magic when we let the silence embrace us. We start to pay attention to the little nudges from our intuition that point us in the right direction. When there are no outside distractions, we learn to tune into our inner wisdom and understand our desires, concerns, and dreams more fully. We can find the solutions we are looking for in this calm as if the cosmos is whispering straight to our hearts.

The ability to heal and restore is likewise possessed by silence. As we practice self-care in our alone time, the burden of the world begins to lighten off our shoulders. We should take this opportunity to renew our spirits and find comfort in life's simplicity. We sometimes feel exhausted from the daily grind, yet stillness is a balm that feeds our souls and restores our energies.

*Dilasha Adhikari*

Adopting silence can seem contradictory in today's environment where noise is frequently praised. We may be afraid of stillness because it forces us to face our thoughts and feelings head-on. However, growth and change can only occur within this suffering. We set out on a voyage of self-discovery by leaning into the quiet, removing the layers to unveil our genuine essence.

Additionally, silence has the capacity to strengthen our bonds with other people. We may create a space where others feel seen and heard when we learn to listen without interruption or judgment. Our presence serves as a light of compassion and comprehension. The most meaningful connections can sometimes be made when we share silent moments that go beyond the bounds of language.

*Dilasha Adhikari*

Cultivating stillness in a noisy world takes effort and repetition. Create a few little periods of solitude each day, to begin with. Indulge in a solitary pastime that makes you happy, find a peaceful area in nature or practice meditation. It's natural for your mind to wander, so have some patience with yourself. All you have to do is come back to the present and once more willingly accept the power of stillness.

There is a strength in the silence that is difficult to find in the bustle of daily life. It is a strength that supports us, gives us power, and enables us to go through the world more purposefully and with more clarity. Accept the calm, treasure the peaceful moments, and allow the power of silence to lead you on your path to self-awareness and inner peace.

*Dilasha Adhikari*

# Creating a Balanced Life: Integrating Solitude with Social Engagement

Finding balance can frequently seem like an elusive task in our fast-paced and connected society. Both physically and digitally, we are always distracted. We may experience exhaustion and a disconnection from our genuine selves as a result of the pressure to be constantly accessible and connected.

But today, I want to welcome you on a trip to live a balanced life—a life where solitude and social interaction coexist together, nourishing our spirits and strengthening our relationships with one another.

*Dilasha Adhikari*

As crucial as isolation is, it's still critical to appreciate the benefits of social interaction. Being social creatures, our relationships with other people have a big impact on how we live. They give us a sense of community, assistance, and shared experiences. Our social contacts help us to grow, learn, and empathize. Human connection has the capacity to inspire us, elevate our spirits, and make us happy.

Look for meaningful relationships that reflect your goals and ideals. Be in the company of people who inspire you, who help you grow as a person, and who support your sincerity. Participate in discussions that are insightful, where ideas are shared and perspectives are broadened.

*Dilasha Adhikari*

In order to achieve balance, one must be present during times of connection and listen to others with genuine interest. Distractions abound in today's culture, making it simple to be physically present yet mentally absent. Develop the skill of active listening by giving those you interact with your undivided attention and empathy. Give up the need to check your phone or think about something else all the time. You honour the wonder of human connection by fully committing to the present.

But remember that finding equilibrium is a dynamic process. As we manoeuvre through the ups and downs of life, it necessitates constant assessment and modification. Seasons may inspire us to enter the world with open arms or may call for deeper seclusion. Accept the fluidity of this dance and rely on your gut instinct to direct you to what your soul really needs.

*Dilasha Adhikari*

Always keep in mind that you have the ability to control your own story as you set out on your path to build a balanced existence. You have the power to make self-care a priority, to establish boundaries that safeguard your well-being, and to foster relationships that improve your life. Accept solitude as a source of strength and allow social interaction to serve as the thread that weaves love and connection throughout your life.

May you discover the delicate balance between solitude and social interaction—a balance that respects your genuine self, feeds your spirit, and strengthens your bonds with others.

May you move through this world with grace, genuineness, and a keen awareness of what makes you happy and fulfilled.

*Dilasha Adhikari*

# Encouragement and guidance to embark on Your own solitary journey

I want to encourage each and every one of you to go out on your own solo journey—a course of personal development, progress, and transformation. You can explore the depths of your existence and get in touch with your genuine nature on this voyage, which offers endless possibilities. I offer you direction and support as you proceed along this route so that you can negotiate the terrain ahead.

Allow yourself to feel the solitude's calm quietness. Let your feelings out, whether they be joy or sorrowful tears. Accept the vulnerability that comes with looking deeply within yourself since it is in accepting our weaknesses that we discover our genuine strengths.

Dilasha Adhikari

This journey is not about running away from the world; rather, it is about going deep within yourself to find the wisdom and love that are already there. It is about taking back your authority, releasing yourself from other people's expectations, and reigniting your own authenticity.

Let nature be your guide as you stroll around the vast, deserted terrain. Admire the beauty of the universe while standing beneath a starry night sky. To be reminded of the interconnectedness of all things, pay attention to the wind's whispers as it dances through the trees. Let nature's beauty inspire you and serve as a reminder of the strength and beauty you already possess.

*Dilasha Adhikari*

You should be aware that the journey to solitude is not a lonely one. You'll meet other travellers along the journey, similar spirits looking for peace and self-awareness. Converse with one another about your experiences, thoughts, and challenges because it is through communication that we gain comfort and power. Together, let's build a place where we can encourage and inspire one another, a place of support and understanding.

I encourage you to accept isolation as a transforming instrument for your personal development. Enter this path with courage, for it is the lonesome trip that will reveal the limitless reserves of love, joy, and knowledge that are within you. Put your faith in the process, let things take their course, and let solitude be your light.

*Dilasha Adhikari*

# Author's Message To Readers

Ever spend a calm evening sitting by a window? As dusk falls, you are left alone. Just you, no hurry, no noise. You begin to understand yourself better at this point. Memories appear like familiar faces. Good and challenging ones. They make up your story like parts of a puzzle.

I start to wonder, "Who am I?" What do I desire? What frightens me? These inquiries are crucial. They open up doorways within you. You discover your passions and aspirations. You confront your worries as well. When you're by yourself, they're not as terrifying.

*Dilasha Adhikari*

It's not lonely to be alone. It resembles a heart-to-heart conversation with your thoughts. You can contemplate while hearing your own breath. You resemble an entire universe. And those dreams you hid from others? They emerge for play. You can bring them to life.

The solitude acts as a teacher. You can learn from it. It says, "You're amazing, just be you." You may see from it that being alone yourself is similar to talking to your own heart. You get used to enjoying your own company. It's like discovering a hidden garden within.

Thus, those moments when you're alone? Keep them close. They serve as mirrors, revealing who you really are.

In reality, you are not alone. You're with the best company - YOU.

*Dilasha Adhikari*

I wish you a Journey of deep self-discovery, unshakable self-love, and unending growth. May you emerge from the loneliness glowing brightly as the personification of your truest self.

*Dilasha Adhikari*

# Acknowledgments

My heart thrills as I prepare to share "The Solitude Code" with the world. I am experiencing a dizzying array of emotions. Without the unfailing love and support of those who have stood by my side, this journey—which was created out of the depths of my personal struggles—would not have been possible.

I'd like to praise my amazing self for having the bravery to walk through life's darkest passageways.

I've been moved to write these words by your tenacity, persistence, and refusal to give up. I will always be grateful to you for demonstrating to me the human spirit's power.

*Dilasha Adhikari*

Thank you for your never-ending support to my family, who stood by me and never wavered in their faith. Your love and support have been my haven, giving me the strength I needed to keep going.

Thank you to the readers who are travelling on this adventure with me for opening your hearts to the pages of "The Solitude Code." Your desire to walk beside me confirms the connection between our shared human experiences.

And to my former self, the one who survived the pit and came out wiser and stronger, I say, "Thank you for enduring, for seeking consolation, and for refusing to let the pit define you." You've set the road for recovery, development, and the birth of this book via your suffering.

*Dilasha Adhikari*

We are all on this trip together, I realize as I write these acknowledgements. We have experienced each tear that has been shed, every obstacle that has been surmounted, and each success that has been celebrated. "The Solitude Code" is a celebration of the inner power we all possess and a monument to the light that can appear in the darkness.

With a heart full of gratitude and love,

Dilasha Adhikari

When you find who you are,
you won't need to find others
in your life,
because
Finding yourself means never
needing to seek others to
complete your life's story.

*Dilasha Adhikari*

> Healing is a Journey that begins with self-love and ends with self-discovery.
>
> — Dilasha Adhikari

Copyright © [2023]

All rights reserved. No part of this publication may be reproduced, distributed, or transmitted in any form or by any means, including photocopying, recording, or other electronic or mechanical methods, without the prior written permission of the author, except in the case of brief quotations embodied in critical reviews and certain other noncommercial uses permitted by copyright law.

www.ingramcontent.com/pod-product-compliance
Lightning Source LLC
Chambersburg PA
CBHW042125100526
**44587CB00026B/4183**